Ghosts

PEGGY J. PARKS

THE LIBRARY OF
Ghosts & Hauntings

ReferencePoint Press®

San Diego, CA

©2010 ReferencePoint Press, Inc.

For more information, contact:
ReferencePoint Press, Inc.
PO Box 27779
San Diego, CA 92198
www.ReferencePointPress.com

Picture credits:
Cover: IStockphoto.com
Maury Aaseng: 62
AP Images: 8, 12, 17, 27, 34, 38, 43, 57
Fortean Picture Archives: 67
Landov: 6, 19, 22, 48, 52

Series design and book layout:
Amy Stirnkorb

LIBRARY OF CONGRESS CATALOGING-IN-PUBLICATION DATA

Parks, Peggy J., 1951-
  Ghosts / by Peggy J. Parks.
     p. cm. -- (The library of ghosts and hauntings)
  Includes bibliographical references and index.
  ISBN-13: 978-1-60152-090-6 (hardback)
  ISBN-10: 1-60152-090-5 (hardback)
  1. Ghosts--Juvenile literature. I. Title.
  BF1461.P37 2009
  133.1--dc22
                                                    2009006176

Contents

Introduction

The Unexplained

Becky Vollink was devastated after her husband died unexpectedly in 2001—but she found comfort in an unusual way. Her daughter, Emma, had always been "Daddy's little girl." Because she was only two years old, Emma was too young to understand the concept of death and constantly asked where her father was, often wandering aimlessly through the house as though she were searching for him. When Vollink took Emma to the funeral home, she expected her daughter to run up to the casket and tell her dad to wake up as she had so many times when he was sleeping in his bed—after all, he did look as though he were asleep. This time, though, Emma refused to go near him. Vollink explains, "She completely ignored him and that shocked me. Of course she could see him lying there, but she wouldn't have anything to do with him. It was like she knew that wasn't her dad anymore, that his spirit was gone—although how she would know such a thing I have no idea."[1]

Later, at home, Vollink was cuddling with Emma on the couch when all of a sudden the child broke into a huge smile, stretched her little arms toward a corner of the room, and exclaimed, "Da Da! My Da Da!" As grief stricken as Vollink was, she found herself overcome with

a sense of calm and peace. "He was there in that room with us," she says, "and I knew it beyond any doubt. I couldn't see him but it was obvious that Emma could, and I strongly felt his presence. I can't even explain how I felt at that moment—like he was comforting us, telling us that we were going to be okay. And I believed him. He was taking care of us just as he always had."[2]

Vollink's story is just one of thousands that people have related over the years. For centuries humans have told of encounters with ghosts, often saying that the mysterious apparitions were either the spirits of dead people that had not yet moved on to the afterlife or were spirits that, for whatever reason, had returned from it. Many claim that they have seen the ghosts of loved ones, but others speak of seeing and talking to the spirits of strangers. These sorts of ghostly encounters are described in many different ways, from comforting and enjoyable to terrifying. Ghosts have been said to be playful and whimsical, such as slamming doors at random, moving furniture around, or yanking curtains open after they are repeatedly closed.

Other experiences have led people to believe that the ghosts they saw were angry, even evil, and had the desire to frighten or harm people. James Van Praagh, who is the cocreator of the television series *The Ghost Whisperer*, says that he has been able to see and communicate with ghosts since he was a toddler. He shares his thoughts:

Did You Know?
Many people feel the presence of their deceased relatives. Sheila Allsup of Modesto, California, says that her mother's ghost is still with her seven years after her funeral.

James Van Praagh, who helped create the the popular television series *The Ghost Whisperer*, says he has been able to see ghosts and communicate with them since he was young. He views ghosts as helpful entities.

When most of us think about ghosts, we tend to clump them into the same category with werewolves, vampires, and zombies. Ghosts are not ghouls who roam graveyards at midnight looking to scare people out of their wits. This perception couldn't be farther from the truth. Granted, ghosts want to communicate with us, but mostly they want to help us, not scare us.[3]

However they are described, ghosts have always been a mystery. Do they really exist? Are they simply a figment of overactive imaginations, or are people's eyes and ears playing tricks on them? Even the most hardened cynic cannot answer those questions with any certainty. Some are highly skeptical about ghosts or any paranormal phenomena, meaning occurrences that fall outside the realm of rational and logical thought. Others are open to the possibility that ghosts exist even if they have never actually seen any. For the many people who say they have had firsthand ghostly encounters, there is no question that ghosts are real. "I guess the only way anyone can understand is if they experience it for themselves," says Vollink. "After all, we're only human—who can say there aren't things that are beyond what we know and believe? I think it's arrogant of us to assume that."[4] From Vollink's perspective, as well as the numerous others who share her views, there are just some things that science cannot explain.

Firm Believers

Whether they are called ghosts, apparitions, ghouls, or spirits, people all over the world have believed in these mysterious entities throughout history. In his book *Ghosts: The Illustrated History*, the late British author Peter Haining speculates that believing in ghosts dates as far back as the Stone Age, but the first detailed descriptions of ghosts were written many centuries later by the Greeks and Romans. Today, the belief that ghosts are real is every bit as strong as it was centuries ago, perhaps even stronger because of worldwide paranormal societies, ghost-hunting conventions, and the popularity of television reality shows such as *Ghost Hunters* and *Haunting Evidence*. According to a November 2008 Harris Interactive poll, 44 percent of respondents said they believe in ghosts, 39 percent did not, and 17 percent were not sure. Although many insist that believing in ghosts is nonsense, plenty of others disagree. And because there is no way for science to either prove or disprove the existence of ghosts, whether they are real or imagined is largely a matter of personal opinion.

Ghostly Encounters

Patrick Burns believes that ghosts are real because of personal experience. A paranormal investigator and cohost of *Haunting Evidence*, Burns reports having his first ghostly experience when he was 10 years old, and he says he has

Reports of ghosts brought Grant Wilson (left) and Jason Hawes to Savannah, Georgia. The ghost-hunting team, known for their *Ghost Hunters* television show, sets up digital recording equipment at the site.

had many more since then. One occurred when he was 21, a year after his brother Billy was killed in a car accident. Burns says that he woke up and could hear Billy's voice in the next room, chatting with an uncle who had died several months before. "I couldn't for the life of me tell you what they were talking about," says Burns. "It was something completely trivial. . . . Just a couple of guys sitting there talking with each other." Burns was terrified. He closed his eyes and waited, and after the talking stopped, he could feel Billy's presence next to him. He was still shaken, as he explains: "I wanted to find some reassurance that Billy was in a good place. I wasn't ready to see him or experience him."[5] By the time Burns felt courageous enough to open his eyes, the ghosts of Billy and his uncle were gone.

Burns shares a more recent encounter that he says occurred late at night when he was working at his computer on a documentary about ghosts. Suddenly he "felt a very pronounced poke with a very large finger, or possibly a paw, just above my beltline on the back." Being accustomed to ghosts because of what he does for a living, Burns ignored it and kept working. He says that the temperature in the room suddenly plummeted and he heard a loud thud, as though a body had slammed into the wall, and the impact was strong enough to shake the house. "I throw off my headphones and say, 'Okay you have my attention now,'" he says. "After that, nothing else happened. It just wanted me to acknowledge that it was there."[6]

Earthbound Spirits

Like Burns, Mary Ann Winkowski is convinced that ghosts exist; in fact, she says she sees them everywhere she goes. She refers to them as earthbound spirits that, for various reasons, are stuck on Earth rather than crossing over to the afterlife. In her book *When Ghosts Speak*, Winkowski describes many of her ghostly encounters, saying that some remain earthbound because they want to make peace with their families over unresolved issues, and others want to watch over their children or other loved ones to protect them. And some, according to Winkowski, remain on Earth because they just want to spy on people, as she explains:

> Those nosy folks who just can't bring themselves to depart are perhaps the most harmless of all earthbound spirits—at least in

terms of intentions. They don't mean to hurt anyone; they stay simply because they're curious. You know the type—the neighbor who is always peeking through your windows, the one who improbably shows up outside to water her gardens and chat every single time you pull your car into the driveway, the guest at the party who goes through the medicine cabinet. These spirits just can't believe they've been handed a free pass to snoop into whoever's life interests them at any given moment.[7]

As Winkowski talks with ghosts, she tries to persuade them to cross over by walking into what she calls "the light,"[8] which she says she has the ability to create.

Winkowski's experience is that most ghosts are harmless, but some remain earthbound because of anger, resentment, or jealousy. Those, she says, are often harder to persuade to walk into the light because they are stubborn and are determined to achieve whatever goal it is that they have set for themselves. "Most often these are folks who are nursing a grudge—sometimes decades old," she writes. "These ghosts are fully aware of the discord they are causing, but are usually getting a sense of satisfaction from making the existence of the living as miserable as their own ghostly existence."[9]

Because Winkowski has built a reputation on being able to communicate with the dead, law enforcement agencies often contact her to help them solve crimes. On one particular case she worked with two officers, Dennis and Sal, from the Drug Enforcement Administration (DEA). About three years later, Winkowski woke up one night from a deep sleep and was shocked to see a man standing at the foot of her bed. She asked him who he was, and he answered, "It's me. Sal. The DEA agent." She put on her glasses, immediately recognized him, and asked what had happened. He spoke rapidly, as though he did not have much time, and explained that he had been working undercover to investigate a drug ring. When the dealers discovered his true identity, they killed him. "Listen, Mary Ann," he said, "they're going to try to dump my body. I need you to call my partner so he can get there right away. Tell him where my body is. My wife—she's going to want it." He gave her the location of his body as well as Dennis's phone number and the names of the criminals. After adding, "Tell him this, too. Tell him I want these guys bad,"[10] Sal's ghost disappeared. Winkowski did as he asked. Even though it was 2:30 A.M., she telephoned Dennis and relayed the information to him. Sal's body was found exactly where he said it would be, and his murderers were later captured. Winkowski attended Sal's funeral, and she says his ghost was there and thanked her over and over for what she had done.

"Grandma Wants Her Ring"

Winkowski and others who specialize in the paranormal say that children are particularly open to the existence of ghosts and may be able to see or sense things that adults cannot. She says parents often assume that a child has an imaginary friend, but that is not necessarily true. "Most children who claim to see imaginary playmates are told to hush, to stop imagining, to grow up, to act like a big boy or girl," she writes. "When people ask me about whether or not children can see spirits, I now tell them that experience has taught me that imaginary playmates are not always imaginary, and children chatting away at a tea

Mary Ann Winkowski firmly believes that ghosts exist, and she has written about her many ghostly encounters. Winkowski often speaks with ghosts in hopes of guiding them toward the afterlife.

party for invisible guests may actually be talking to spirits only they are aware of."[11]

The Atlantic Paranormal Society (TAPS) experienced this in August 1999. The group was contacted by Louis and Delia Taylor, who said their four-year-old daughter was having an ongoing conversation with her grandmother. Because the older woman had died several months before, the Taylors initially believed that the child was imagining the whole thing. But they reconsidered because she seemed to know details that she could only have heard from her grandmother. TAPS interviewed the little girl, whose name was Selena, and she told them that "Grandma" said she was not in the house to harm or frighten the family but rather to watch over them. Selena added that her grandmother had not crossed over into the afterlife because she "just wasn't ready."[12]

The TAPS team left the Taylor home and returned a few days later with a psychic medium, whom they hoped would be able to communicate with the ghost. They gathered in Selena's bedroom, and the medium said she could feel the ghost's presence. Selena then began talking to her grandmother and relaying messages back to her parents. Suddenly the child jumped up, walked out of the room, and headed downstairs to the basement, with the group following behind. They watched with curiosity as she dug through some cardboard boxes that were stored at the end of a room, pulled out a small wooden box, looked past them as though she could see someone standing there, and asked, "Is this the box, Grandma?" Then, as if hearing her grandmother say yes, Selena opened the box, dug through a stack of old photographs, pulled out a diamond ring, and then handed it to her mother, saying, "Grandma wants her ring."[13] Everyone who witnessed it was stunned.

Afterward the group discussed the matter, and the Taylors decided to go to the cemetery where the woman had been buried, dig a hole over her coffin, and bury the diamond ring there. The following week the TAPS team called them and learned that they had gone to the grave-site and had buried the ring as planned—and after that, Selena no longer saw or heard her grandmother's ghost.

Returning from the Light

Those who specialize in the paranormal say that occurrences such as Selena's are not uncommon. Once earthbound spirits (such as Selena's grandmother) have reconciled whatever business they have with the living, they

Did You Know?
Mary Ann Winkowski says ghosts cannot read minds unless they had that ability when they were alive.

find peace and can finally cross over into the afterlife.

James Van Praagh says that he sees ghosts on a regular basis, but he cannot see earthbound spirits. Rather, those he sees have already gone into the light and have personal reasons for revisiting Earth. In many cases, they return because they want to comfort grieving family members and assure them that even though they no longer have physical bodies, they are still very much alive. According to Van Praagh, once spirits have crossed over, they are blissfully happy and feel "an overwhelming sense of being free." As he explains, "Not once when doing my work have spirits ever said to me that they wished they could come back to earth and live again. The spirits with whom I communicate are usually thrilled that they are in the light and would want it no other way."[14]

He adds that unlike earthbound spirits, which can be restless, troublesome, and even evil toward humans, the ghosts he sees are always gentle and kind. "Ghosts walk among us," he writes, "impressing us with their love, guiding us with their wisdom, and protecting us from harm."[15]

In his book *Ghosts Among Us*, Van Praagh writes about using his abilities to help ghosts communicate with their grief-stricken families. He says this occurred a few years ago when he agreed to meet with a young woman named Candy, who was extremely distraught and had been referred to him by a friend. While they were sitting together in Van Praagh's living room, he told her that he could see two men standing nearby: "There's an older gentleman behind you. I feel it is a father figure. He is mentioning something about being from Scotland and has a slight Scottish accent. He has a black-and-white sheepdog named Sharkey." Candy appeared to be stunned and burst into tears, saying that her father was

indeed Scottish and proud of his heritage, and Sharkey had been their family dog. Van Praagh felt that there was more to tell her, and he continued: "I'm picking up on a young man with your father who keeps on talking about 'Blue Thunder.' Your father wants you to know that he helped this young man cross over. ... He says his name is David. He is dressed all in white and is showing me a wedding ceremony. He seems to be somewhere tropical like Hawaii."[16]

Candy began to cry harder, and when Van Praagh gently asked if David had been her fiancé, she said yes. He had been a professional race-car driver who was killed when his car, *Blue Thunder*, had spun out of control and crashed on the track. They had been engaged and had planned to marry in Hawaii. Van Praagh was convinced that David had appeared to comfort Candy, to let her know that the afterlife was wonderful and he would be waiting for her so they could someday be together again.

The Ghost of Aunt Vern

Van Praagh and other paranormal specialists say it is common for ghosts that have not yet crossed over to attend their own funerals, often because they are curious about what sorts of arrangements have been made, who is in attendance, and what people are saying about them after they are gone. But there are also accounts of people at funerals who encountered the ghosts of other relatives who died years before. Rochelle Kunard experienced this when she was at the funeral of an uncle who had died of cancer. She walked into the church, and as she approached the podium on which the guestbook rested, Kunard saw her aunt Vern standing nearby. She was glad to see her aunt because even though they used to get together for

The Gangster Ghost

In 1929 the infamous Chicago gangster Al Capone (also known as "Scarface") orchestrated the St. Valentine's Day Massacre, in which seven rival gang members were killed. Capone was never convicted of the crime, but a few months later he was arrested and sent to Eastern State Penitentiary for carrying concealed weapons. While he was in prison, he insisted that he was haunted by the ghost of James Clark, one of the gangsters who had been killed in the massacre. Other inmates heard Capone screaming during the night, begging "Jimmy" to go away and leave him alone.

After Capone was released from prison, he continued to insist that Clark's ghost was haunting him and that it followed him wherever he went. Author Rosemary Ellen Guiley explains, "Capone's men often heard Capone begging the ghost to leave him in peace. Several times, his bodyguards thought he was under genuine attack and broke into his room." Capone became so desperate that he consulted with a medium by the name of Alice Britt, who tried to get rid of the ghost but was not successful. Capone became convinced that the ghost of

While imprisoned in this cell at Eastern State Penitentiary, gangster Al Capone complained of being haunted by the ghost of a rival gang member.

James Clark "would literally follow him to his own grave"—and up until his death in 1947, he believed that Clark had done exactly that.

Rosemary Ellen Guiley, *Encyclopedia of Ghosts and Spirits*. New York: Facts On File, 2009, p. 81.

annual family reunions, they had not seen each other for a long time. The two greeted each other warmly, and then, because Kunard had arrived a bit late for the service, she signed the guestbook and told her aunt that she needed to go inside and take her seat. Aunt Vern nodded and said, "Okay. It's good to see you, Rochelle."[17]

After the service was over, Kunard chatted with relatives at the luncheon. She spotted her mother across the room and walked over to her. "Mom," she said, "just before the funeral service I saw Aunt Vern! We only talked for a few minutes but it was great to see her after all this time." Kunard's mother hesitated for just a moment and then spoke quietly to her daughter: "Rochelle . . . Aunt Vern died a couple of years ago."[18] Kunard was not aware of her aunt's death, so she was taken aback at first. But then she knew, without a doubt, that it was Aunt Vern's spirit she had talked to at the funeral home.

Her mother, who specializes in the spiritual healing method known as Reiki, is very open to the possibility of paranormal occurrences, and she told Kunard that her brother had also seen and spoken with their aunt at the funeral. "Is there an explanation?" asks Kunard. "Of course not . . . well, at least not in the 'logical' sense. But what does 'logical' mean, anyway? That anything that can't be seen or heard according to scientific principles is all there is? Sorry, but I don't buy that. I *saw* my aunt at the funeral. My brother *Saw* my aunt at the funeral. We both talked to her. And our mom accepted this without question."[19]

"A Gray Area"

People often hotly debate the issue of whether ghosts exist. Because there is no way their existence can be proved in a scientific laboratory, skeptics say the lack of evidence is enough to show that they are not real. But believers

Did You Know?
There have been many reports of dogs and cats becoming agitated as though they could see or sense the presence of ghosts.

A Reiki practitioner places her hands over a client's body. Reiki is a relaxation and healing technique that focuses on what practitioners call "life force energy." Some experts attribute paranormal events to a similar type of energy.

disagree—especially those who say they have actually encountered ghosts and have talked to them. Researcher and author Rosemary Ellen Guiley says that in order to gain a better understanding of what is called "the unknown," it is important to examine objective data provided by science as well as subjective data that comes from people's paranormal experiences. She writes, "Yes, I believe ghosts are real. They exist. I believe ghosts exist from my own experiences and from the weight of historical testimony and supporting evidence. Can I prove ghosts exist? No. But skeptics cannot disprove ghosts either. When it comes to the paranormal, we are in a gray area with very few defined markers."[20]

CHAPTER 2

Ghostly Hauntings

Homes, hotels, lighthouses, and other structures that are said to be haunted have fascinated people for centuries. Although nonbelievers reject the notion that any place could be haunted, many people swear it is true because of their own personal experience. Troy Taylor, founder of the American Ghost Society, says that even though science cannot prove that hauntings actually occur, a tremendous amount of evidence exists that should not be ignored.

Taylor cites one example of a family that moved into a home (he does not say where) and began to observe strange happenings, such as doors opening and closing by themselves, lights flicking on and off, and objects vanishing only to reappear several days later in odd locations. In addition, the family saw what appeared to be the ghost of a man in a back hallway. They decided to contact the previous owners and were astonished to learn that they had witnessed the same strange occurrences, including seeing the ghostly man, but they had chosen not to tell anyone. "Checking back even farther," Taylor writes, "they discovered that other owners had shared these same experiences. Before this, no one was aware that others had seen the same things, and they had never been discussed outside the family. Scientifically, no one had proven that a ghost was haunting this house, but there is *historical evidence* of this fact."[21] Taylor adds that, when looking through old photos, all the witnesses identified a picture of the original owner of the house as the ghost they had seen—and they each did it separately, without knowledge that other residents had picked out the same photograph.

The Ghost Stalker

Mary Ann Winkowski agrees that ghosts can, and do, haunt many different places. She says that these earthbound spirits often remain attached to sentimental objects such as jewelry, furniture, or the homes they lived in, and it is difficult for them to let go and cross over. She experienced this during her first meeting with Jennifer Love Hewitt, who stars in *The Ghost Whisperer*, a television show that is based on Winkowski's life. At the beginning of their conversation, Love (the name she prefers) asked if there were any ghosts in the room, and Winkowski answered that there were two, a young man and a woman. Upon questioning the female ghost, Winkowski learned that she was the ex-wife of the actor Lon Chaney Jr., and she was in Love's house because she used to live there. Winkowski says that the ghost was smiling, and after having a pleasant conversation, she created the light and the female ghost was happy to go into it.

The young man was a different matter, and Winkowski had an uneasy feeling about him from the first glance. Although he answered her questions candidly, she says he had a constant smirk on his face. "If I'd met him when he was alive," she writes, "I'd have called him a creep. Dead, he was no different."[22] Upon talking with him, she learned that he had gone to high school with Love and had been a longtime admirer of hers. He explained that he was killed in a collision, and now that he was a ghost, he was able to watch her day and night, even when she took a shower. Winkowski says that she scolded him for his behavior, made the white light, and watched him walk into it.

Actress Jennifer Love Hewitt (left) confers with Mary Ann Winkowski during filming of *The Ghost Whisperer*. The popular television series was inspired, in part, by Winkowski's experiences with ghosts.

During a meeting the following day, Love told her that the man's name sounded familiar to her so she had called some of her girlfriends from high school. One of them said that after he had died, his parents went into his room to clean it and found that he had plastered an entire wall with photographs of Love. Winkowski shares what went through her mind upon learning that: "*It makes sense. . . .* The guy was literally a stalker when he was alive. How much easier had it been for him once he was dead?"[23]

A Mischievous Ghost

Ghosts like the one that stalked Love are said to be petulant and annoying but not necessarily frightening. The same could be said about Nick, a ghost that is widely believed to have taken up residence in a theater at Kansas State University. Although there are conflicting stories about who Nick was when he was alive (or even if he existed at all), many believe that he was a football player at the college during the 1950s who was severely injured on the field. He was taken to the cafeteria immediately afterward, where he died, and that is the current site of the theater. People have reportedly heard Nick stomping through hallways, up and down stairs, and on the theater's stage. The ghost is known for playing pranks, such as turning off the theater lights, fiddling with the heat, hiding theater props, moving objects around in dressing rooms, piling chairs and boxes on top of each other, and dumping buckets of paint on the floor.

Kay Coles, a former theater major at Kansas State, relates one occurrence that involved Nick's ghost. A crew had just finished unloading chairs in the theater and planned to set them up later. The men had left the theater, but they ran back inside when they heard a

Did You Know?
A June 2005 Gallup poll showed that 37 percent of Americans believed in haunted houses, 46 percent said they did not, and 16 percent were not sure.

commotion. They were astounded to find that the chairs had all been set up and there was a program placed neatly on each seat. "There was nobody around," Coles says. "It happened in five minutes, and it usually takes at least half an hour to do the job."[24]

She says that Nick also played a trick on her and another student after they had turned off the theater's sound system one night and had locked the theater. Once they were outside they could hear music playing, and when they went back in to investigate, they found that the tape was running. Mystified, they turned it off, locked the doors, and left—and again they heard the music. "It (the machine) came on four more times," says Coles. "We looked around for someone playing a joke, but there wasn't a soul around."[25] They were convinced that it was Nick's ghost up to his usual tricks to which people had grown accustomed over the years.

"Who Stole Ossian?"

Kansas State University is not the only college where ghosts are said to dwell. The Roy O. West Library at DePauw University, located in Greencastle, Indiana, is reportedly haunted by the ghost of James Whitcomb, who served as the governor of Indiana from 1843 to 1849. Whitcomb was an avid collector of books, and one of his prized possessions was entitled *The Poems of Ossian, the Son of Fingal*, which had been given to him as a gift when he was a young boy. Upon Whitcomb's death he bequeathed his entire collection of rare books to the DePauw library, stipulating that they were to remain there and never be allowed to leave the building.

As the story goes, during the late 1800s a boy went to the library and became thoroughly engrossed in *The Poems of Ossian*. When the library closed he had not finished reading the book, so he slipped it in his pocket and took it home. It was well after midnight when he finally tucked the book under his pillow, turned out the light, and went to sleep. Later something woke him up, as authors Beth Scott and Michael Norman explain:

> Suddenly he was awakened by what . . . a sound? Someone knocking at his door? His eyes slowly focused. At the foot of his bed hung a spectral body draped in dark, musty clothing. A skeletal arm reached toward the boy, its bony finger pointed accusingly. "Who stole [Ossian]?" Over and over it moaned the title of the book hidden beneath the student's pillow. The ghost lashed out toward the quivering figure on the bed, its bony hand actually touching the boy's face. . . . An eternity later, or so it seemed to the young victim, the figure faded away.[26]

First thing the next morning, the shaken boy returned the book to the library, confessing to the librarian what he had done and telling her that the ghost of Governor Whitcomb had visited him in the night. He promised that he would never again remove a restricted book.

Over the years there have been numerous reports of strange shadows and unexplained happenings on the library's second floor, where Whitcomb's books are housed. His collection is now kept in a locked area of the library, where only librarians have access to *The Poems of Ossian* and other rare volumes, and many are convinced that his ghost lingers there, watching over his books and protecting them.

The Haunted Lighthouse

Although no one can explain what happened in the De Pauw library, whether it is actually haunted is not known. The same may be said of the lighthouse in St. Augustine, Florida, which is often called one of the most haunted cities in the United States. In January 2006 a TAPS team went to investigate the lighthouse, and cofounder Jason Hawes describes their impression at seeing it for the first time: "Even from a distance, the lighthouse's tower sent chills up and down our spines. It had red and white stripes like a gigantic candy cane, but there was nothing sweet about it. You got the feeling there was something creepy going on inside."[27] TAPS investigators learned that during the 1870s, when the lighthouse was being built, the two young daughters of the construction supervisor had drowned in the surrounding waters. Many people, including lighthouse employees, claimed that they had heard the girls' ghosts talking and running on the stairs, and there were reports of other ghostly encounters as well, such as a ghostly woman who tended to appear during severe storms.

As the investigators climbed the tall, winding staircase that led to the top of the lighthouse, they began to observe strange phenomena, including footsteps and sounds of people talking. Hawes says they could hear a little girl's voice, a man and woman having a conversation, and then a child who was jabbering. He explains:

> The voices seemed to be coming from farther up the tower, so we ascended the stairs. It was then that we saw something walk by a window, blotting out the light— not once, but twice. It looked like the head and shoulders of a man. And it seemed to

St. Augustine Florida's lighthouse (pictured with a former keeper) is reported to be haunted by ghosts. Among them are the ghosts of two young girls who drowned while the structure was being built. The lighthouse, which was originally red and white, has since been repainted black and white.

be moving up the stairs, just as we were. We started moving up the stairs again, hoping to catch up with whatever we had seen. Then something stopped us cold. It was a human silhouette, not more than ten feet away. And it was leaning over the railing, looking down at us.[28]

Other members of the team told Hawes that they had heard a woman moaning and asking for help. "Running up the stairs," he writes, "they saw something grab the handrail and look down at them. Then it seemed to disappear—and reappear a level closer to them. It was as if the thing was coming down, not running away from them. Then they saw a small explosion of light and the figure vanished."[29] According to Hawes, some of the team members were so frightened by what they had observed that they refused to go back into the lighthouse. A camera operator was badly shaken after his headphone was removed from one of his ears and someone (or some-*thing*) whispered to him.

During the investigation the TAPS team took video footage and captured some of what they had seen and heard on tape. Afterward they reviewed it and could clearly see the shadow at the top of the stairs and could hear the woman crying for help. They showed it to the lighthouse's director of education, who had never believed any of the stories about the structure. But after watching the video, Hawes says that the color drained from his face and he told them, "That lighthouse is haunted."[30]

A Restless Resting Place
Many people are also convinced that Bachelor's Grove Cemetery is haunted. Located in a suburb of Chicago,

The Haunted Battlefield

In July 1863 one of the bloodiest battles of the Civil War took place in Gettysburg, Pennsylvania. It lasted for three days, and when it was over, thousands of Union and Confederate soldiers had been killed and tens of thousands of others died afterward. In the years since, numerous people have reported seeing and hearing ghosts. As a result, Gettysburg is often called one of the world's most haunted cities. Witnesses have said they have heard screaming, the sound of gunfire and cannons, and strange music, and many have reported seeing the spirits of soldiers, dressed in uniform, wandering around the former battlefield. Sue Norton claims that while she was standing in the area, she was physically "swept back" by the force of thousands of people. Since that time Norton has been fascinated by the story of Gettysburg. As she explains, "The energy here, it's unmatched."

Buildings in Gettysburg, such as the Jennie Wade House Museum, are also said to be haunted by Civil War ghosts. The museum is named after Mary Virginia Wade, who at the age of 20 was the only civilian killed in the battle. She had been baking bread in the kitchen of her sister's home when a bullet passed through two doors and struck her in the back, killing her instantly. People visiting the museum have reported incidents such as rocking chairs that rock back and forth even when no one is sitting in them, chains rattling, mysterious voices, and the smell of bread baking. Others have sworn that they saw the ghost of Jennie Wade herself, sometimes accompanied by a young boy.

Quoted in Erin James, "Travel Channel Set to Capture Gettysburg's Ghosts," *Evening Sun*, October 9, 2008. www.eveningsun.com.

Bachelor's Grove is more than 150 years old. There have been over 100 reports of strange phenomena, from a glowing man to the ghost of a lady carrying a baby in her arms. People have also reported flashing and dancing white and blue lights, a brilliant red light that moves through the air and leaves a streak behind it, vehicles that appear and then vanish, and a white Victorian farmhouse with pillars in front that fades away whenever someone moves toward it.

During the late 1970s two patrol officers who were on night duty near Bachelor's Grove reported seeing an old man who was steering a horse-drawn plow. They stared in shock as they watched the apparition emerge from a pond, cross the road in front of their vehicle, and then disappear into the forest. Since that time, numerous others have reported seeing the ghostly man and plow, and many believe that it is the ghost of a farmer whose land was once where the cemetery is now. Legend has it that during the mid-1800s the farmer was plowing a field by the pond when something spooked his horse, causing the animal to bolt into the water. According to Troy Taylor, the farmer became tangled in the reins and could not free himself. Unable to get out from under the heavy plow, both he and the horse drowned.

Because of the numerous ghostly sightings that have been reported throughout the years, Bachelor's Grove Cemetery is a popular place for paranormal investigators to visit. In August 1991 a team from the Ghost Research Society went to the cemetery to take photographs in the hope of capturing ghostly phenomena on film. One of the investigators, Jude Huff, was using high-speed infrared film to shoot a panorama of an area that was said to be especially active with unexplained occurrences. After her pictures were developed, one showed the misty fig-

ure of a young woman, wearing an old-fashioned white dress, sitting in a relaxed pose on a tombstone. Because Huff had not seen the mysterious figure while she was taking pictures, she assumed that the camera had captured the image of a ghost. After the photo was published in the *Chicago Sun-Times*, skeptics said that it was a fake that had been created through double exposure, which occurs when a photographer superimposes one image onto another. But when Taylor took the picture to several professional photographers, he says that they ruled out double exposure. Today, according to Taylor, the photo remains unexplained.

The Mysteries Linger

From mansions to theaters, and from lighthouses to cemeteries, tales of ghostly hauntings abound throughout the world. Are these stories real? Is it possible that ghosts take up residence somewhere and then proceed to haunt their surroundings? Nonbelievers would emphatically say no; because ghosts do not exist, it is not possible for them to haunt anything. They may be correct, but how does one explain such phenomena as the ghostly figures in the St. Augustine lighthouse? Could everyone who claims to have witnessed Nick's mischievous antics in the Kansas State theater be imagining the experience? No one knows the answers to these questions. Just as there are many skeptics, there are also numerous others who *do* believe. Taylor shares his thoughts: "Today with new technology assailing us on every side, scientists continue to assure us not to worry—there are no ghosts, no hauntings, and no haunted houses. In the cold light of the modern era, such things cannot exist. There is nothing out there, lurking in the night. However, we know different, don't we?"[31]

CHAPTER 3

Flying and Floating Ghosts

Ghost stories typically revolve around creaky old mansions, haunted hotels and inns, and spooky cemeteries. But in his book *The World's Most Haunted Places*, author Jeff Belanger says that ghosts are often sighted in other sorts of places. He writes that "ghostly legends abound in ancient castles, old homes, and historic battlefields, but the supernatural is by no means only tied to land."[32] Indeed, there have been numerous accounts of mysterious occurrences on ships and airplanes, and the people who say they witnessed these happenings are convinced that what they saw was not a figment of their imaginations. Even if they are ridiculed or accused of lying (which happens often), many are still willing to share their stories with others.

The Ghosts of Flight 401

Some of the most intriguing ghost stories have been told by former pilots and flight attendants who worked for Eastern Airlines, especially those who flew on a jumbo jet known as plane 318. Reports of mysterious encounters began surfacing in the aftermath of a disaster that occurred in 1972. Eastern Flight 401, another jumbo jet that was carrying 13 crew members and 163 passengers, crashed into the Florida Everglades just before midnight on December 29. More than 100 people died in the crash, most on impact and others shortly afterward, and among the dead were captain Robert Loft and second officer Donald Repo.

Not long after the crash, crew members on plane 318 began to notice weird, inexplicable happenings. On one trip from Newark, New Jersey, to Miami, flight attendant Sis Patterson (not her real name) was doing her usual preflight head count in the first-class section when she found that the number was off by one. A recount showed no change, and then Patterson noticed a uniformed Eastern Airlines captain sitting in one of the seats. It was not uncommon for crew members to catch flights back to their home bases, but they always checked in before boarding, and this officer had not done that. Patterson walked over to him and asked his name, but he ignored her. She noted that he was staring straight ahead with a dazed look on his face. She tried again. "I beg your pardon, captain, I've got to check you off either as a jump-seat or first-class pass rider. Could you help me?"[33] He still did not look her way, nor did he respond to her. Another flight attendant, whom Patterson asked to speak with the officer, was also unsuccessful at getting his attention. Feeling perplexed, the two women went into the cockpit to get the captain. He approached the unidentified officer, leaned down to speak to him, and froze in place, exclaiming, "My God, it's Bob Loft!"[34] Then, according to airline personnel who later recounted the story, the mysterious captain vanished—in full view of the three crew members and other first-class passengers.

Repo was reportedly seen on plane 318 even more often than Loft. On a flight from New York to Mexico City, a flight attendant was preparing food carts downstairs in the galley. She glanced toward the window of one of the ovens and could clearly see a man's face staring back at her. Shocked, she ran to the elevator, punched the

Years after the crash of Eastern Airlines Flight 401, visitors arrive at the Florida Everglades crash site by airboat to commemorate those who died there. For many years, crews on other flights reported seeing Flight 401's captain and second officer on their planes.

button, rode it to the main floor cabin, and grabbed another flight attendant, whom she asked to go down to the galley with her. When they arrived, the second flight attendant looked at the oven and she, too, saw the face. They called the flight deck and talked to the flight engineer, who agreed to come to the galley immediately. When he got there, he looked at the oven and saw exactly what the other two had seen—and just before the face vanished, the engineer recognized it as Repo's. After the bizarre incident, none of the three had any idea what to make of it.

Plane 318 landed in Mexico City, and its next destination was Acapulco. When the captain was preparing for takeoff, he found that one of his 3 engines would not start. Although mechanics who examined the engine determined that it needed to be replaced, the captain was authorized to fly the plane because it was designed to run on only 2 engines. The captain took off, and the aircraft began its ascent. But when it had reached an altitude of only 50 feet (15m), a second engine stalled and then backfired, necessitating that it immediately be shut down. The captain discharged fire retardant to keep the engine from bursting into flames, managed to increase altitude enough to circle around, and then successfully guided the plane back to the runway, where he landed without any problems. Later the 3 crew members who had seen Repo's face in the oven glass said that just before he vanished, he had warned the flight engineer, "Watch out for fire on this airplane."[35]

Many other strange incidents were reported on plane 318 as well, such as one that occurred on a flight bound from New York to Miami. When the plane was over the Everglades, a male voice came over the public address system and made the routine announcement about fastening seatbelts and preparing for landing—but according to crew members, the public address system was off at that time and no one from either the cockpit or cabins had made the announcement. In an equally puzzling instance, a flight engineer was checking an engine's

hydraulic system when a uniformed man approached him and pointed out exactly where the problem was. It was only after the man had disappeared in front of his eyes that the astonished engineer realized he had been talking to Repo's ghost.

A strange story recounted by flight attendant Emily Palmer (not her real name) involved a female passenger on plane 318 who was seated next to a quiet man dressed in an Eastern Airlines uniform. She thought the man looked unusually pale and was perhaps ill, but when she asked him if he was all right, he did not answer her. She called the flight attendant, who asked the man if she could help him, and she, too, got no response. Then, in full view of the small group observing the incident, the uniformed man reportedly vanished. The female passenger became hysterical, and when the plane arrived in Miami she demanded to see photos of Eastern Airlines officers. When she saw Repo's picture, both she and the flight attendant identified him as the man they had seen in the first-class cabin.

Upon hearing the peculiar accounts stemming from the December 1972 Eastern Airlines crash, author John G. Fuller began an investigation for a book he was writing entitled *The Ghost of Flight 401*. During his research he interviewed numerous people, including crew members on Eastern and other airlines. One was an Eastern pilot who told Fuller that after the wreckage of Flight 401 was retrieved from the Everglades, salvageable components, such as galley ovens, radios, and other electronic equipment, were pulled from the plane, rebuilt and tested, and then installed on working aircraft, including plane 318. Fuller theorized that this was likely the cause of the mysterious occurrences—that the ghosts of the Flight 401 officers had attached themselves to the salvaged equip-

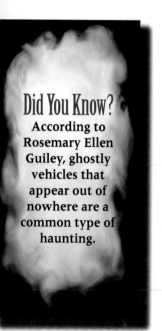

Did You Know?
According to Rosemary Ellen Guiley, ghostly vehicles that appear out of nowhere are a common type of haunting.

ment and were still hanging around it. Eastern Airlines officials vehemently denied that there were ghosts on any of their aircraft, but Fuller learned that mechanics were ordered to remove all parts salvaged from Flight 401 and used on other planes, even if they were in perfect working order.

The Haunted *Hornet*

Although some insist that the mysterious occurrences on the Eastern flights could not possibly have happened, many of the reported witnesses were officers, flight attendants, and other reputable professionals who say they had nothing to gain by making up the stories. The same is true of those who reportedly witnessed ghostly happenings on the USS *Hornet*, an aircraft carrier that was in commission from 1943 to 1970.

The USS *Hornet*, which is as large as three football fields, was the U.S. Navy's most decorated ship, earning nine battle stars for service during World War II. But like all aircraft carriers, it was a dangerous place for crews to work. In the steam room, for instance, if a pipe ruptured it released a blast of super-heated steam that could instantly kill crew members who were standing anywhere near it. Another dangerous area was the catapult, a device that resembled a monstrous slingshot and could shoot planes off the ship's deck and send them flying into the air. If the catapult's cable accidentally snapped, it spun around with a force powerful enough to slice through anything or anyone in its path. At least three crewmen were decapitated when their necks were struck by the out-of-control spinning cable. Although the USS *Hornet* accomplished many victories over its 27 years of service, hundreds of men died while working on the ship, either through tragic accidents, acts of war, or suicide.

Did You Know?
Phantom travelers that appear and then suddenly vanish have been reported on airplanes, trains, and ships.

Since 1995 the USS *Hornet* has been docked at Alameda Naval Base in Alameda, California, and it is now a national historic landmark and museum. During the time that it has been docked, numerous paranormal occurrences have been reported by museum employees as well as by tourists, and many are convinced that the ship is haunted by the ghosts of military crewmen who served on it.

The USS *Hornet*, one of the Navy's most decorated ships, is now a museum. Museum employees have reported many unexplained occurrences, including odd voices, footsteps, falling objects, opening and closing doors, and a wandering headless sailor.

There have been reports of odd voices and footsteps, doors opening and closing on their own, objects falling off shelves and rolling across the floor, and radios and other nautical instruments turning on and off at random. One visitor who was using the restroom said she felt someone (or something) smack the back of her head, and others have said they were punched or grabbed by unseen beings. A number of people have reported seeing uniformed sailors and officers appear before them and then suddenly vanish. Even the curator of the museum, former U.S. Navy Sea, Air, Land (SEAL) team member Alan McKean, had a ghostly encounter. As he explains, "I'm not a true believer in all of that stuff. But I saw what I saw. One day I saw an officer in khakis descending the ladder to the next deck. I followed him, and he was gone. I have no explanation for it."[36] One ghost that has been particularly frightening to those who say they have seen it is a headless crewman. Thought to be the ghost of one of the sailors who were decapitated by the catapult cable, the ghostly crewman, wearing a uniform, has reportedly been spotted wandering around the ship as if he were lost.

Did You Know?
Visitors to the former Navy ship USS *Constellation* have reported ghosts that looked so realisti that they were mistaken for costumed tour guides.

The Ghosts of the *Queen Mary*

Like the USS *Hornet*, the RMS *Queen Mary* is also docked in California, but it is a very different kind of ship. The *Queen Mary* is a luxury cruise liner that traveled the North Atlantic Ocean. From its maiden voyage in 1936 until its retirement in 1967, the ship made more than 1,000 crossings. During World War II the *Queen Mary* was used to transport military troops, as well as prisoners of war, around the Pacific and Indian oceans. Thousands of troops were crowded onboard at once, and because the ship had been designed to travel the colder Atlantic rather than tropical areas, no air conditioning was ever installed. The ship grew unbearably hot during these long journeys, and as a result, many onboard the *Queen Mary* died of heat-stroke before ever reaching their destinations. As psychic Peter James explains, "Fact has it that troops were dying at a rate of one every 7 minutes for hours. That's how bad it was, because they were packed like sardines."[37]

Hundreds of other military troops died as the result of a horrendous crash that occurred in 1942, when the *Queen Mary* was on one of its war missions. As it was steaming along at full speed, being escorted through hostile waters by a smaller vessel called the HMS *Curaçao*, the smaller ship inadvertently crossed its path. Unable to stop, the massive ocean liner slammed into the *Curaçao*, slicing it in half. More than 300 crew members died, either as a result of the collision or by drowning.

Since the *Queen Mary* has been docked in Long Beach, California, it has been turned into a first-class floating hotel with restaurants and banquet facilities—and it has also become known for its hauntings. According to James, "The *Queen Mary* is the most haunted place that I have ever investigated. And I've literally been around the globe with hauntings. This is number one as the most haunted place in the world. There are at least 600 active resident ghosts on the *Queen Mary*."[38]

Many are convinced that the majority of these "residents" are the ghosts of military troops who died either from heatstroke or from war wounds. It is also believed that ghosts of the victims of the 1942 *Curaçao* crash have taken up residence on the ship. James contends that "to this day, you can hear the collision—the residual sound effects and also the water splashing and many screams for help."[39]

A number of nonmilitary ghosts have also been said to

The Ghost of Deke Slayton

On the morning of June 13, 1993, a bright red Formula One racing plane took off from John Wayne Airport in Southern California. People watched as the plane performed fancy maneuvers in the sky, but because its high-speed propellers made so much noise, they wrote down its N21X registration number and reported it to the Federal Aviation Administration (FAA). After its performance, the plane steadily climbed in a westerly direction and then disappeared from sight. Upon investigation, the FAA determined that the aircraft, which belonged to retired astronaut and racing-plane pilot Deke Slayton, had exceeded decibel levels mandated by law. Officials sent a citation letter to Slayton saying that he had broken the law.

After the letter arrived at Slayton's home, his wife telephoned the FAA and asked officials if they had lost their minds. She told them that her husband had died on June 13—*six hours before* he had allegedly been sighted—and his plane had been housed in an aviation museum, with its motor removed, since the previous March. According to paranormal specialist Loyd Auerbach, this phenomenon shows "that the spirit of the space program, embodied in Deke Slayton, can truly survive even the most impossible situations, even death."

Loyd Auerbach, "Of Moon Shots and Ghost Astronauts," Paranormal Network, 2008. www.mindreader.com.

haunt the *Queen Mary*. During the years when the ship was operating as a luxury liner, travelers died because of medical conditions, accidents, or by drowning in one of the two swimming pools. According to communications director Robin Wachner, employees have observed a mysterious man dressed in black who appears out of nowhere and then vanishes. As she explains, "People have walked over to see if they can help this man, and he's just gone." Wachner says there have been other peculiarities as well: "We also have a lot of instances within our offices of doors just mysteriously opening and closing when there's no wind and no windows open. There have been some strange happenstances aboard the *Queen Mary* among the employees—people see disembodied heads, legs, and images, and people dressed in vintage clothing disappear into thin air."[40]

Another commonly reported sighting on the *Queen Mary* is the ghost of John Pedder, an 18-year-old fireman who worked on the ship and was crushed to death by a watertight door in 1966. Witnesses have said that they heard unexplained knocking around the door, and others have reportedly seen a darkly dressed figure leaving the area where Pedder was killed. After looking through old photographs, the witnesses identified the ghost they saw as Pedder.

Many visitors to the *Queen Mary* have reported hearing the sounds of laughter and water splashing around the ship's two swimming pools, and some have reported seeing people dressed in old-fashioned swimsuits. This is particularly mysterious because both of the pools were drained years ago and are now closed to all guests except those taking guided tours.

James says that he frequently encounters the ghost of a little girl named Jackie, who drowned in one of the

The luxury liner *Queen Mary* completes its final voyage at sea in 1967. Now a floating hotel and museum, the ship was previously used to transport troops during World War II. It is said to be haunted by the ghosts of sailors and crew members who died at sea, as well as passengers who died while traveling on it.

pools when she was four or five years old. He has seen Jackie many times, and whenever he calls out to her, she answers in a voice that sounds like a little screech. California resident Tony Mellard, who has taken James's ghost tour several times, says that he has personally witnessed the ghost girl's voice, and James adds that more than 100 others have heard it as well. On one of the tours, a woman asked James if she could give Jackie a doll as a gift, and he agreed. She put the doll, which had a long ribbon tied around its neck, on the floor by the old pool. Then she called out Jackie's name and started running her video camera. James explains what happened next: "She panned her camera back, and all of a sudden on video—and I have a copy of it—the ribbon began to come undone. And it was completely pulled off the doll by Jackie."[41]

Truth or Fiction?

No one can explain the occurrences on the Eastern Airlines flights, the USS *Hornet*, or the RMS *Queen Mary*. Ghosts have appeared to thrive in all three locations, and numerous accounts have supported this. Could the reported sightings be chalked up to coincidence, human imagination, or even outright lying? Or is it possible that the ghosts really do exist and the people involved are relating what actually happened? The answers to those questions may remain elusive forever.

CHAPTER 4

In Search of Ghosts

On the evening of October 24, 2007, paranormal investigator Christopher Moon was at the Prosperity School Bed and Breakfast in Joplin, Missouri, at the request of its owners, Richard and Janet Roberts. The couple told Moon that the old schoolhouse had stood empty for 30 years before they purchased it in 2002, and they had heard many stories about its past. People in the area were convinced that the building was haunted, and the Robertses noted numerous peculiar occurrences since they had moved in and refurbished the inn. Guests had reported seeing shadowy figures passing by windows, having a strong sense that there was a ghostly presence nearby, strange knocking and clanging sounds, and doors that mysteriously opened on their own. One guest, a retired schoolteacher, said that she could hear the voices of children reciting their multiplication problems. Another guest told of a book flying off her bed. The Robertses had strange experiences of their own, such as televisions and lights turning themselves on and off, shadowy figures, lightbulbs exploding, and their dog howling as though it could sense someone or something near its crate. Because of so many unexplainable happenings, the Robertses asked Moon to come to the inn and see what he might be able to find.

Ghostly Conversations

Accompanying Moon to the Prosperity School Bed and Breakfast was a group of students from Missouri State University who were interested in paranormal phenomena and wanted to watch him work. In his hands he held an instrument that he called a "Telephone to the Dead," which was designed to serve as a two-way communication device between the living and the spirit world. Moon spoke into the instrument. "Are you there?" he asked. "Where are you?" At first there were no sounds except for static, but the students gathered around Moon and listened carefully. Then a sound came from the box. According to Moon, it was a little girl's voice that said, "I'm saying my prayers." Everyone in the group was shocked, and Moon continued: "What's your name, sweetheart?" After a long period of more static, she answered, "Sadie." Moon asked her how long she had been there, and she said, "Seems like forever. Help, I'm tired."[42] No one except Moon could understand what the voice was saying, so he interpreted it for them. He says that he has the ability to hear spirits talk, and then he relays their messages back to the living. He told the Robertses that Sadie had died in 1906, when she had fallen down the stairs, and that she and five other spirits inhabited the inn.

Moon's so-called Telephone to the Dead was built by Frank Sumption, an engineer and shortwave-radio enthusiast. Often called "Frank's Box," the device scans AM and FM radio frequencies continuously, creating white noise that Moon and many others believe can allow spirits to communicate with the living. Since Moon acquired the device, he has used it in hundreds of investigations, and he says it has allowed him to have numerous conversations with members of the spirit world.

Did You Know?

Paranormal investigators often hear ghostly sounds and voices on tape that were not audible during an investigation.

Patrick Burns uses a different type of instrument to communicate with spirits. Known as an Ovilus, the small, handheld device works by measuring changes in environmental factors, such as temperature and electromagnetic activity. It then translates these phenomena into recognizable words. During one paranormal investigation at an old theater in Savannah, Georgia, a psychic medium in attendance said that she sensed the spirit of a young man about 22 years old standing near the aisle. Burns walked over to where the psychic pointed, set the Ovilus down on the floor, turned on the switch—and nearly collapsed from shock when he heard a robotic-sounding voice say, "Brother Billy." His brother had been 22 when he was killed, and Burns was convinced that his spirit was attempting to communicate with him. He began asking questions: "Billy, can you affect this device? Can you speak to me?" After a long period of silence, Burns asked, "Billy, do you have a message for mother?" The voice spoke again but the random words seemed to make little sense to Burns, until it uttered: "Tender . . . . Smile. . . . Sorry" and then "Rest. . . . Mother. . . . Happy." Those words seemed to indicate that Billy was trying to comfort family members who were left behind when he had died more than 20 years before. When the Ovilus was finally silent, Burns reached down and, with a shaky hand, shut the device off and then said, "Whoa. That was . . . wow. Just wow."[43]

Ghost-Hunting Tools

The Ovilus is just one of many instruments that paranormal investigators use in their line of work. In an article titled, "8 Tech Tools Every Ghost Hunter Needs," writer Kevin Hall says that many of these tools are commonly available, "letting you start your search for the

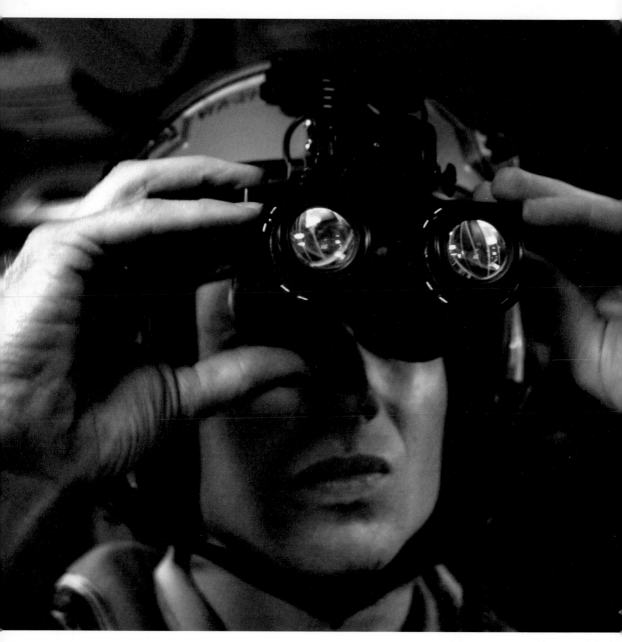

Ghost hunters use a variety of tools to document and monitor ghostly activity. Night vision goggles (demonstrated here by a naval aviator) are one of several high-tech tools favored by some ghost hunters.

paranormal as soon as you get home from Best Buy. From infrared cameras to night goggles, high-tech gear comes in real handy when dealing with the ethereal backlog of human history, not to mention otherworldly spooks."[44]

According to Hall, a .35mm camera is valuable on ghost-hunting expeditions because film is easier to enlarge when an image is processed, which means tiny details that could possibly be paranormal phenomena may be spotted. Also, ghostly phenomena captured on film is more credible because digital photos are much easier to fake. Hall does, however, recommend a digital infrared camera for capturing apparitions that may be invisible to the human eye. Other instruments Hall recommends are a digital video camera for capturing moving images, a digital thermometer to measure sharp temperature changes, a field recorder that measures fluctuations in electromagnetic fields (EMFs), and night-vision goggles because, he writes, "given the creepy nature of hauntings, many ghosts won't want to come out until it's good and dark. You don't want to stumble around when candlesticks are flying across the hallway."[45] A thermal-imaging digital camera also comes in handy because it allows an investigator to visually see hot and cold spots and how they affect the environment around them when spirits are present.

Did You Know?
When the term *ghost hunter* is typed into the search engine Google, millions of pages are displayed.

Joe Nickell is a paranormal investigator who does not use high-tech tools. As he explains, "Why would we even be taking EMF detectors when we have no scientific evidence that they detect ghosts?"[46] Nickell prefers to use the scientific approach, gathering evidence in much the same way that detectives gather evidence at the scene of a crime. He starts by having witnesses fill out a "ghost questionnaire" that addresses factors such as what sort of phenomenon they observed, how often they observed it, and what time of day and/or night it happened. He takes photographs at the scene, and if he finds anything that could be a potential sign of ghostly activity, he uses a forensic evidence kit to take samples, which he analyzes in his laboratory. In one case that he investigated at a Kentucky farmhouse, the owners reported that whenever it rained, blood dripped from one of the doors. Nickell gathered samples of the substance, and when he analyzed them, he found that the "blood" was nothing more than rust and other materials washing off the roof with rainwater and then dripping off the door.

Nickell often finds logical explanations for things that are mistaken for paranormal activity, and in his many years of investigating he has never encountered a single ghost. Yet even though he is a known skeptic, he does not completely rule out that such entities exist. Rather, he is critical of those who assume that they *do* exist without adequate evidence. "In scientific inquiry one seeks to gather, study, and follow the evidence, only positing a supernatural or paranormal cause when all natural explanations have been decisively eliminated," he explains. "Investigation seeks neither to foster nor debunk mysteries but instead to solve them."[47]

Although Jason Hawes and his partner, Grant Wilson, are more amenable to the existence of ghosts than Nickell and have reported numerous paranormal encounters, they also believe in the scientific approach. Hawes writes:

> Most groups in search of the paranormal are only too happy to embrace "evidence" when they find it. T.A.P.S. is different. We examine that evidence five ways to Sunday,

looking for a way to disprove it—to show that it's attributable to a breeze, or a reflection, or some other normal, everyday phenomenon. And the more spectacular the finding, the more eager we are to find an explanation for it. It sounds masochistic, I know. But that's how we've established a reputation for credibility.[48]

"The Holy Grail"

Hawes and Wilson disagree with Nickell on the use of high-tech equipment during investigations. Whenever they go on a ghost hunt, their team is armed with a virtual arsenal of instruments, including digital video recorders, cameras that are designed to work in total darkness, thermal-energy cameras, and remote cameras, among other instruments. In June 2005 TAPS investigators traveled to Eureka Springs, Arkansas, to visit the Crescent Hotel. Built in 1886, the Crescent Hotel and Spa was once known as America's most luxurious hotel, but over the years it waned in popularity and eventually became a boarding school for young women. In the 1930s the building was converted into a medical facility by Norman Baker, a man who deceived people into thinking he was a doctor and who claimed to have developed a cure for cancer. "Taking the life savings of desperate cancer patients, Baker subjected them to cruel and outlandish methods that had no chance of working," Hawes explains. "In the end, his patients all died, some of them in terrible pain without the benefit of anesthesia."[49] The Crescent Hotel has been completely refurbished, and today it is again a luxurious resort—one that is widely believed to be haunted.

The TAPS team was invited to check out the Crescent

Hotel by the general manager and Eureka Springs's town historian. The investigators learned that paranormal activity had been observed throughout the hotel, such as in room 212, where guests reported seeing a man dressed in Victorian clothing exit the elevator, cross the hall, and enter room 212 by going through the door without opening it. Paranormal happenings were also reported in the kitchen, where a cook said he walked in early one morning, flipped on the lights, and watched in shock as pots and pans started flying off their hooks. An area that was said to be especially haunted was the basement morgue where Baker used to perform autopsies. In a back room of the morgue, Hawes and Wilson discovered a series of numbered lockers.

Wilson set up a thermal-imaging camera and began scanning the lockers when he saw something startling. He rewound the camera and showed it to Hawes, who says they could "clearly and unmistakably [see] the figure of a man rendered in gaudy thermal colors, less than six feet from Grant and the camera. And the figure was looking back at Grant, as if it was as curious about him as we were about *it*. When I saw what my partner had captured, my mouth went dry."[50]

Hawes adds that the figure was wearing some kind of hat, perhaps a Civil War soldier's cap, and a number 2 was emblazoned on its sleeve that was a bright, fiery red as though it were burning. The team did not see anything else for the rest of the night, and they packed up their equipment and left just before dawn. But they were excited about what they had observed, as Hawes says: "We had stumbled on a full-body apparition, the Holy Grail of the ghost-hunting field!"[51] Although it does not happen very often, Hawes and Grant declared that the Crescent Hotel was indeed haunted.

OPPOSITE: Ken Fugate (left) and Carroll Heath lead nightly ghost tours at the Crescent Hotel (in the background) in Eureka Springs, Arkansas. Now a luxury resort, the hotel once served as a boarding school for girls and later as a clinic for a disreputable doctor.

Spooky Voices

Although no one has officially declared the DePauw University library to be haunted, many unusual occurrences have been reported over the years. As a result, a ghost-hunting team from Hoosier State Paranormal wanted to investigate the library. The group's founder, Chris Lien, asked the archives and special collections official if they could visit. He agreed but only gave them permission to stay for one hour. The team went to the library on January 20, 2009, after it had closed for the evening, armed with infrared cameras, thermometers, digital recorders designed to pick up voices and other sounds that are inaudible to the human ear, and EMF detectors.

Because they were on a tight schedule, they quickly set up their equipment in the archives room so they could begin their investigation. According to Lien, only a few minutes passed before they observed a flash of light moving down a computer screen on the table where *The Poems of Ossian, the Son of Fingal* was sitting. They marked the time down and then noticed that their thermometers had caught an extreme temperature change in a back office where an antique chair sat. With their recorders running, the investigators moved around the room asking Whitcomb to talk to them, with one saying in a sarcastic voice, "Where are you, Mr. Governor, you don't scare us!"[52]

Other than the flash of light and the thermometer's reading, the team noticed no other unusual activity— but when they got back to their office and listened to their recordings, what they discovered made them ecstatic. Lien says they had picked up two electronic voice phenomena (EVP) immediately after the question, "Where are you, Mr. Governor?" had been asked. On the recording was a man's voice saying, "I've been

Did You Know?
Since 2004 viewership of the reality television show *Ghost Hunters* has doubled, growing from 1.3 million viewers to 2.6 million in 2008.

The Myth of the Spirit Phone

Thomas Edison was a world-famous scientist who invented the electric lightbulb and the phonograph as well as hundreds of other items. Numerous Web sites, articles, and essays state that Edison was interested in building an instrument known as a spirit phone that would facilitate communication with the dead. Edison, as it turns out, had no such interest. But the story did not grow out of thin air. Its origin is actually with the inventor himself.

Edison was interviewed by journalist B.F. Forbes for an October 1920 magazine article. During the interview Edison remarked that if humans could "evolve an instrument so delicate as to be affected, or moved, or manipulated . . . by our personality as it survives in the next life, such an instrument, when made available, ought to record something." Edison told Forbes that he was working on building a prototype of the machine, and newspapers all over the world ran the story. Only later did Edison admit that he had made the whole thing up. The curators of the Thomas Edison National Historic Site say they have more than 5 million pages of Edison's documents archived, and not even one mentions such an instrument.

Alex Boese, "Thomas Edison and His Spirit Phone," Museum of Hoaxes, 2008. www.museumofhoaxes.com.

dead," and then shortly afterward, "I'll be back." The Hoosier team says that they cannot confirm with certainty that Whitcomb is haunting the college library, but they can "confidently say that there is something paranormal in the archives."[53]

Patrick Burns and his team of paranormal investigators have also recorded EVP during some of their ghost-hunting expeditions. In October 2004 Burns was asked by a man named Jeff Tate to visit his 100-year-old home in Athens, Georgia. According to Tate, before his mother died she told him about an incident that took place late in her life. One evening, when she was feeling upset, she looked up and saw Uncle York, a man who had worked on her grandfather's plantation when she was a young girl. When she saw the man, who had died decades before, he looked exactly as she remembered him and was smiling at her. She called out, "Uncle York, Uncle York,"[54] but he didn't speak; instead, he just continued smiling at her and then faded away. Her son explains his mother's reaction: "She interpreted his smile as meaning whatever was worrying her would go away and it was gonna be OK. And the story ends there."[55]

Burns and paranormal investigator Christine Parks began walking around Tate's house while filming with a video camera and running a digital recorder. "Would anyone like to speak to us tonight?" Burns asked as the recorder was running. "We mean no disrespect by being here tonight. We're simply looking for a sign of an afterlife. We'd appreciate it if you could speak for us. Give us a sign you're here."[56] They heard nothing while they were in the house, but after running through the tape later, they found that the recorder had picked up EVP. Burns says that they could hear laughter and what

A TAPS technician sets up a digital infrared camera in preparation for a ghost investigation. Audio recorders and thermal imagers will also be used. A thermal image (inset) shows views that would not normally be seen with the naked eye.

sounded like children giggling in the attic. Also, coming from an old stairwell in the basement, they could hear an unidentifiable sound that resembled a cry.

Who You Gonna Call?

Burns, Hawes, Wilson, and many other paranormal investigators are dead serious about their work, and their goal is to solve the riddles posed by mysterious phenomena that no one is able to explain. Quite often they find perfectly logical reasons for strange happenings—but not always. In their pursuit of the unknown, ghost hunters are well aware that they are operating outside of traditional science. As Hawes writes, "We understand that ghost hunting isn't an exact science. We have to accept the fact that we're working in a real-world setting. However, we're determined to come as close to scientific accuracy as we possibly can. That's the only way we're going to produce reliable evidence and advance the study of the paranormal."[57]

What Else Could It Be?

Those who are convinced that they have witnessed paranormal occurrences, or who believe that their homes are haunted, are often not open to the idea that there could be a logical explanation for what they have experienced. They steadfastly hold on to the belief that what they saw and felt was real, and they are disappointed, or even furious, if anyone challenges them. As Patrick Burns explains:

> This is one of the problems we run into. There is a very strong desire for people to be able to believe or have evidence that we survive, that we live on. A lot of people desperately want their house to be haunted. They don't want a mundane explanation such as poorly shielded wiring or a medical condition. This has become almost a status symbol to some people. People want to say, "My house is haunted."[58]

Paranormal or Environmental?

Burns's mention of wiring is in reference to an investigation he performed during 2007 at a home in Augusta, Georgia. A family telephoned Ghost Hounds, the paranormal investigation group founded by Burns, to report seeing dark apparitions moving throughout the house. Burns arrived at the home, and after talking with the family to gather information, he began walking around with an EMF detector. When the device's needle shot deep into the red zone, Burns knew that he was close to a powerful magnetic field. He investigated the home's crawl space and discovered a large, suspended chunk of wiring that was unshielded, meaning there was not a conductive barrier to limit the flow of electromagnetic fields. Because electromagnetism would be especially strong in the area where unshielded wires were located, Burns suspected that this was the actual cause of what the family had experienced rather than paranormal phenomena. He told them about the faulty wiring and the effects it could have on them, but they refused to accept his theory and remained convinced that their house was haunted. He says they still believe that today.

People often mistake electromagnetic fields in their homes for ghostly presences. Some are extremely sensitive to EMFs, and this sensitivity can lead to physical ailments such as dizziness or even hallucinations. As a result, they may see shadows and sense ghostly presences that are not actually there.

According to psychology professor Michael Persinger, the sensation that someone might believe to be a paranormal experience is actually a side effect of the two sides of the person's brain trying to work together. His theory is based on the fact that when the brain's right hemisphere (the side that is associated with emotion and intuition) is stimulated in a certain part of the cerebral area, the left hemisphere (the rational, logical side) tries to make sense of the stimulations. Persinger calls this *cerebral fritzing*, and says that it can cause the mind to generate what the person feels is a sense of presence, as

Did You Know?

The human brain sometimes forms shapes or colors into familiar features or patterns. This is termed matrixing and it may explain why people see things that are not really there.

well as almost anything else that could be described as paranormal phenomena. Psychologist Ciarán O'Keeffe explains how this was demonstrated in a study: "Experimental subjects who were exposed to a specific series of pulses from TMS (transcranial magnetic stimulation) described feeling an invisible presence near them or feeling connected to the whole world."[59]

In addition to EMF sensitivity, the sensing of paranormal presences is sometimes caused by low-frequency sound waves known as infrasound. Although humans cannot hear infrasound, they can feel it, and this has been shown to produce negative effects in some people, such as extreme sorrow, anxiety, fear, nervousness, and chills. These physical symptoms could cause a person to feel a great sense of discomfort and uneasiness that could easily be mistaken for sensing a ghostly presence in a room.

Another effect of infrasound is that it can cause people's eyes to vibrate, which can make them see things that are not actually there. In the 1990s Coventry University lecturer Vic Tandy was working in a laboratory when he saw a "gray thing" moving toward him. "I felt the hairs rise on the back of my neck," he says. "It seemed to be between me and the door, so the only thing I could do was turn and face it."[60] The apparition vanished but then it returned in a different form the next day.

Tandy, who is a known skeptic of paranormal phenomena, investigated the strange occurrence. He learned that the "gray thing" was not any sort of ghostly presence but rather was caused by a faulty fan motor that was emitting low frequency sound waves. "When we finally switched it off," he says, "it was as if a huge weight was lifted."[61]

According to TAPS investigator Brannon Osborne,

Did You Know?
Scientists believe that unexplained yellow or white lights known as "ghost lights" are probably just refracted light from vehicle headlamps, ball lightning, or swamp gas.

Cerebral Fritzing

According to one psychologist, the sensation that a person might think is a paranormal experience could be a side effect of the two sides of the brain attempting to work together which can cause a great amount of confusion.

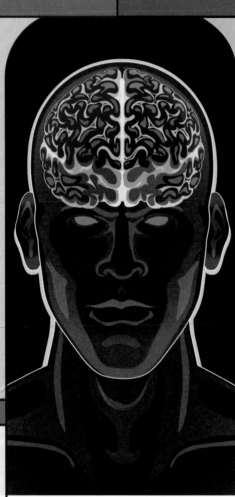

Right Hemisphere	Left Hemisphere
Intuitive	**Rational**
• Responds to demonstrated instructions	• Responds to verbal instructions
• Problem solves with hunches, looking for patterns and configurations	• Problem solves by logically and sequentially looking at the parts of things
• Looks at similarities	• Looks at differences
• Is fluid and spontaneous	• Is planned and structured
• Prefers elusive, uncertain information	• Prefers established, certain information
• Prefers drawing and manipulating objects	• Prefers talking and writing
• Prefers open ended questions	• Prefers multiple choice tests
• Free with feelings	• Controls feelings
• Prefers collegial authority structures	• Prefers ranked authority structures
Simultaneous	**Sequential**
• Is a lumper: connectedness important	• Is a splitter: distinction important
• Is analogic, sees correspondences, resemblances	• Is logical, sees cause and effect
• Draws on unbounded qualitative patterns that are not organized into sequences, but that cluster around images	• Draws on previously accumulated, organized information

Source: Brain Wave Entrainment Technology, "Left vs. Right: Which Side Are You On?" 2005. www.web-us.com.

after the discovery, Tandy visited various sites in England that were reportedly haunted, and found two that had especially high levels of infrasound. He then conducted an infrasound experiment at the Purcell Room, a concert and performance venue in London, England. During a concert, low-frequency sound waves were incorporated into the music intermittently, and the attendees were asked to fill out surveys to record their feelings and emotions at various times throughout the evening. Osborne explains the result: "The research netted an over 20 percent increase in heightened emotions, anxiety, and chills with the infrasound than without. [Lo] and behold, the scientific realm has finally discounted ghost[s] . . . or has it? Out of all the areas that Mr. Tandy visited, he only found two that had infrasonic activity, not all of them."[62] Osborne adds that the concert experiment did not show whether people felt the same heightened emotions when no infrasound was played, so the study's results do not prove that all paranormal phenomena are associated with infrasound.

Brains Playing Tricks

Just as people often disagree about whether ghostly presences are real or are the result of infrasound or other natural causes, another source of controversy is electronic voice phenomena. Many scientists theorize that what people may interpret as voices from the spirit world are actually bits of radio broadcasts, CB radio transmissions, or cell phone conversations that are picked up as the sounds travel through the atmosphere. Yet paranormal investigators who have recorded EVP disagree, saying that the voices they hear often relay messages that are relevant and meaningful to the listener, and some carry on interactive conversations. This, they argue, would be

Did You Know?
Along with faulty wiring, electromagnetic fields are also caused by microwave ovens, power lines, televisions, and computer monitors.

impossible if the voices were merely random sounds. Dave Oester, who cofounded the International Ghost Hunters Society, shares his views: "I have been an amateur radio operator for 40 years, and I have never had tape or digital recorders pick up any artificial interference. Also, how can an interactive EVP, where the spirit is responding to my questions or commenting on my words, ever be considered interference?"[63]

Another scientific theory about EVP is known as apophenia, which occurs when humans perceive patterns or connections among random or meaningless data. York University psychology professor James E. Alcock explains:

> Perception is a very complex process, and when our brains try to find patterns, they are guided in part by what we expect to hear. If you are trying to hear your friend while conversing in a noisy room, your brain automatically takes snippets of sound and compares them against possible corresponding words, and guided by context, we can often "hear" more clearly than the sound patterns reaching our ears could account for.[64]

Alcock adds that people who believe they hear ghosts talking to them may actually be hearing random noise, but they still believe ghosts are speaking because that is what they want, and expect, to hear. He states:

> Of course, if we play the same piece of tape over and over . . . and if we do everything we can to focus our attention on the "noise"

**Did You Know?**
Electronic voice phenomena (EVP) were first discovered in 1959 by a Swedish man who recorded a voice talking about bird songs.

. . . then we not only increase the likelihood of discerning voices if they really are there, but we maximize the opportunity for the perceptual apparatus in our brain to "construct" voices that do not exist, to detect patterns that match up with our expectations.[65]

According to Reese Christian, a psychic and medium who often works on paranormal investigations with Burns and his Ghost Hounds team, another reason why people "see" ghosts is because they believe in them and desperately *want* to see them. This, she says, is often enough for them to assume that ghosts are real, without being willing to listen to any explanation to the contrary. As she explains, "It's almost like if I tell you you're sick. I say it over and over. You start believing you're sick, and then you're going to become sick. It's not that I cursed you, it's that I made you believe it. People can do that with their home. They can believe it's haunted even if there was never any reason to think so. Then they create their own haunting."[66]

Ghost Pictures

One of the most common ways that people report seeing ghosts is by looking at photographs that appear to show spirits. This was the case with Nick Harrigan, who was one of the students who accompanied Christopher Moon to the Prosperity School Bed and Breakfast in October 2007. While Moon was having his conversation with Sadie, he encouraged the students to take photographs in the immediate area. Harrigan used a digital camera to take photos on the staircase, and when he looked at the display he was astounded—there was a blurry white streak in front of the banister that closely resembled an arm. Upon further examination, though, Harrigan determined that the "arm" was actually a stray patch of brightness (known as lens flare) that was likely caused by a ceiling fan on the first floor.

Joe Nickell had a similar experience during the 1970s when he was investigating an alleged haunting at an old inn called Mackenzie House. The caretaker showed him a photograph that showed a peculiar white blur in front of a piano, and it was believed to be one of the inn's resident ghosts. Nickell gave the picture to a professional photographer for analysis. He learned that a bright flash had been used when the photo was taken, which caused a reflection to bounce off sheet music that was lying on the piano; hence, the mysterious blur. This sort of misconception often happens when people scrutinize supposed ghostly visions that show up in photographs. Scientists compare it to staring at clouds and seeing faces or other recognizable objects or forming patterns out of stars in the nighttime sky.

Other phenomena that often show up in photographs are orbs, which are luminous spots of light. Rosemary Ellen Guiley says that orbs range in size from as small as a golf ball to the size of a basketball. "Some are rectangular, diamond-shaped, or like streaks of light," she explains. "Orbs range in color from pale white to yellow to pale blue to red. They may glow and twinkle. Some appear to be transparent or semi-transparent, while others are dense. Some seem to have nuclei within them. Some are in motion and appear to have tails."[67]

Guiley adds that people often get excited when they see orbs, especially when the photos were taken in places that are reportedly haunted, but she says that most orbs are caused by natural phenomena. For instance, a camera's flash may pick up particles of dust, pollen, water droplets, or even insects in the air. There can also be interference from the camera itself. For instance, a lens may be dirty or spotted with tiny drops of water, and the person taking the pictures may not notice these things until the image is developed. On some occasions a camera strap or piece of hair may fall in front of the lens just as the picture is snapped, and this can also result in orbs appearing in photos. According to Guiley, paranormal investigators are typically skeptical of orb photographs and believe that the majority do not represent ghostly images.

Bright spots of light of varying sizes, shapes, and colors sometimes show up in photographs taken at sites where ghost activity has been reported. These orbs (pictured) may have explainable causes. But sometimes no cause can be found.

Psychic or Sham?

John Edward is famous for being a psychic and medium, and he travels the world giving presentations. Edward's critics say that his "revelations" are nothing more than lucky guesses, and he has also been accused of using deceptive tactics. In 2001 a man from New York named Michael O'Neill appeared on the television program *Crossing Over with John Edward* in the hope of hearing from his deceased grandfather. Edward told O'Neill that he had messages from his grandfather, and although some details were correct, many were not. Weeks later, when O'Neill watched the program on television, he noticed some suspicious discrepancies. As journalist Leon Jaroff writes, "Clips of him nodding yes had been spliced into the videotape after statements with which he remembers disagreeing. In addition . . . most of Edward's 'misses,' both on him and other audience members, had been edited out of the final tape."

O'Neill recalled that while the audience was waiting to be seated, Edward's aides were mingling with people and asking them to fill out cards with their name, family members, and other details. Once everyone was inside the auditorium, there was more than an hour delay before the show started, and the crew said it was due to technical difficulties. Jaroff continues, "And what did most of the audience—drawn by the prospect of communicating with their departed relatives—talk about during the delays? Those departed relatives, of course." These conversations, O'Neill suspects, may have been picked up by the microphones strategically placed around the auditorium and then passed on to Edward.

Leon Jaroff, "Talking to the Dead," *Time*, February 25, 2001. www.time.com.

Troy Taylor is one of the skeptics. "Enough with the 'orbs' already!" he writes. "'Orbs' are not evidence of the paranormal. They are not ghosts and they are not even 'unexplained!'" Taylor does believe that a small number of orb photos could be evidence of something paranormal and these should continue to be studied. That is not the case with most of them, however, as he writes: "It's the 'traditional orb photos' that have become the bane of paranormal research and I think that it's time that we retired this irrelevant theory for good."[68]

Yet there are a number of photographs in which spirit visions look startlingly real, and Taylor says that these should not be discounted. His Web site links to several realistic spirit photos for which he says there is no explanation. Some of the photos were taken at Greenlawn Cemetery in central Indiana, where the photographer captured a ghostly figure standing amongst the headstones. At Kemper Hall, a girls' boarding school in Kenosha, Wisconsin, that has stood empty since 1975, photos taken by historian David Schmickel clearly show white-hooded figures in the windows.

One of the most famous photographs for which there is no definitive explanation is the shot of the misty woman sitting on the tombstone that was taken by Jude Huff in 1991. After the photo was made public, an expert from Eastman Kodak examined it and said that because he could see a shadow, it was a real person sitting on the tombstone, not an apparition. Yet according to Taylor, that is not correct. Although objects in the cemetery cast shadows, he says the ghostly woman did not. Another consideration is that when the photo was taken, neither Huff nor the nine other investigators from the Ghost Research Society saw the woman who was pictured. Founder and president Dale Kaczmarek states, "I was there. I know nobody was dressed like that. I know no one there faked the photograph. I know there were several other members at the same time taking photographs of that tombstone with different film, and nobody else got anything. I can't explain that photograph. . . . It was one shot out of thirty-six where anything showed up."[69]

Unknown, Uncanny, and Unexplained

Paranormal phenomena are mysterious as well as controversial. Nonbelievers dismiss the very idea of ghosts as silly or the products of vivid imaginations. Yet even though there is no scientific proof that these entities exist, neither is there proof that they do *not* exist. Although it is true that many so-called paranormal experiences are the result of humans' eyes and ears playing tricks on them, electromagnetic energy, infrasound, or other natural causes, not all ghostly encounters can be so easily explained. The same is true of photographs that show spiritlike figures. Even though many of them have been shown to be fake, or have resulted from natural interferences such as water droplets, dust, or lens flare, others exist for which those criteria do not apply. And what about EVP? Is it caused by radio or cell phone signals bouncing around the atmosphere, or is it the spirit world trying to communicate with the living?

The reality is, people will never agree on these issues. For every person who strongly believes in the paranormal, there is another who chalks it up to nonsense, and this will likely always be the case. Still, there are numerous mysteries for which there are no answers—and that is precisely why they are called *mysteries*.

Source Notes

Introduction:
The Unexplained

1. Becky Vollink, interview with author, December 1, 2008.
2. Vollink, interview.
3. James Van Praagh, *Ghosts Among Us.* New York: HarperCollins, 2008, p. 37.
4. Vollink, interview.

Chapter 1: Firm Believers

5. Quoted in Kimberly Turner, "Haunted," *Atlanta Magazine,* October 2008. www.atlantamagazine.com.
6. Quoted in John Blake, "When Ghosts Attack," CNN, October 31, 2008. www.cnn.com.
7. Mary Ann Winkowski, *When Ghosts Speak.* New York: Grand Central, 2007, p. 17.
8. Winkowski, *When Ghosts Speak,* pp. 102–103.
9. Winkowski, *When Ghosts Speak,* p. 77.
10. Quoted in Winkowski, *When Ghosts Speak,* p. 100.
11. Winkowski, *When Ghosts Speak,* pp. 142–43.
12. Jason Hawes and Grant Wilson, *Ghost Hunting.* New York: Pocket, 2007, p. 56.
13. Quoted in Hawes and Wilson, *Ghost Hunting,* p. 58.
14. Van Praagh, *Ghosts Among Us,* p. 30.
15. Van Praagh, *Ghosts Among Us,* p. 5.
16. Van Praagh, *Ghosts Among Us,* p. 31.
17. Rochelle Kunard, interview with author, January 30, 2009.
18. Kunard, interview.
19. Kunard, interview.
20. Rosemary Ellen Guiley, *Encyclopedia of Ghosts and Spirits.* New York: Facts On File, 2009, p. xii.

Chapter 2: Ghostly Hauntings

21. Troy Taylor, foreword to *Encyclopedia of Ghosts and Spirits,* by Rosemary Ellen Guiley. New York: Facts On File, 2009, p. vii.
22. Winkowski, *When Ghosts Speak,* p. 5.
23. Winkowski, *When Ghosts Speak,* p. 7.
24. Quoted in Beth Scott and Michael Norman, *Haunted Heartland.* New York: Barnes and Noble, 1985, p. 154.
25. Quoted in Scott and Norman, *Haunted Heartland,* pp. 153–54.

26. Quoted in Scott and Norman, *Haunted Heartland*, p. 91.
27. Hawes and Wilson, *Ghost Hunting*, p. 231.
28. Hawes and Wilson, *Ghost Hunting*, p. 235.
29. Hawes and Wilson, *Ghost Hunting*, pp. 236–37.
30. Quoted in Hawes and Wilson, *Ghost Hunting*, p. 239.
31. Taylor, foreword to *Encyclopedia of Ghosts and Spirits*, p. vi.

Chapter 3: Flying and Floating Ghosts

32. Jeff Belanger, *The World's Most Haunted Places*. Franklin Lakes, NJ: Career, 2004, p. 23.
33. Quoted in John G. Fuller, *The Ghost of Flight 401*. New York: Berkley, 1976, p. 167.
34. Quoted in Fuller, *The Ghost of Flight 401*, p. 167.
35. Quoted in Fuller, *The Ghost of Flight 401*, p. 195.
36. Quoted in Dana Hull, "USS *Hornet*—Staff and Visitors Report Seeing & Hearing Strange Things," *San Jose (CA) Mercury News*, August 11, 2000. www.rense.com
37. Quoted in Belanger, *The World's Most Haunted Places*, p. 24.
38. Quoted in Belanger, *The World's Most Haunted Places*, p. 24.
39. Quoted in Belanger, *The World's Most Haunted Places*, p. 25.
40. Quoted in Belanger, *The World's Most Haunted Places*, p. 26.
41. Quoted in Belanger, *The World's Most Haunted Places*, p. 27.

Chapter 4: In Search of Ghosts

42. Quoted in Joe Hadsall, "Ghost Hunter Claims 'Walkie-Talkie' Allows Communication with Dead," CNHI News Service, October 29, 2007. www.andovertownsman.com.
43. Quoted in Kimberly Turner, "Haunted," *Atlanta Magazine*, October 2008. www.atlantamagazine.com.
44. Kevin Hall, "Eight Tech Tools Every Ghost Hunter Needs," DVice, December 28, 2007. http://dvice.com.
45. Hall, "Eight Tech Tools Every Ghost Hunter Needs."
46. Quoted in Ed Grabianowski, "How Ghost Busters Work," How Stuff Works, 2005. http://science.howstuffworks.com.
47. Joe Nickell, "Investigative Files: Ghost Hunters," *Skeptical Inquirer*, September 2006. www.csicop.org.
48. Hawes and Wilson, *Ghost Hunting*, p. 208.
49. Hawes and Wilson, *Ghost Hunting*, p. 209.
50. Hawes and Wilson, *Ghost Hunting*, p. 212.
51. Hawes and Wilson, *Ghost Hunting*, p. 212.
52. Hoosier State Paranormal, "Evidence: Case Files," January 2009. www.hoosierstateparanormal.com.
53. Quoted in Maribeth Ward, "Hoosier State Paranormal Group Investigates

Book at DePauw Library," *Banner Graphic*, January 26, 2009. www.bannergraphic.com.

54. Quoted in Wayne Ford, "Ghost Hunt," *Athens Banner-Herald*, October 31, 2004. www.ghosthounds.com.

55. Quoted in Ford, "Ghost Hunt."

56. Quoted in Ford, "Ghost Hunt."

57. Hawes and Wilson, *Ghost Hunting*, p. 14.

Chapter 5: What Else Could It Be?

58. Quoted in Turner, "Haunted."

59. Ciarán O'Keeffe, "Ghost Hunting Equipment: EMF Meter," Suite 101, October 2, 2007. http//:ghosts-hauntings.suite101.com.

60. Quoted in Robert T. Carroll, "Infrasound," *Skeptic's Dictionary*, January 3, 2009. http://skepdic.com.

61. Quoted in Carroll, "Infrasound."

62. Brannon Osborne, "Infrasound and the Paranormal," Atlantic Paranormal Society. www.the-atlantic-paranormal-society.com.

63. Quoted in Stephanie Watson, "How EVP Works," How Stuff Works, 2005. http://science.howstuffworks.com.

64. James E. Alcock, "Electronic Voice Phenomena: Voices of the Dead?" Committee for Skeptical Inquiry, 2005. www.csicop.org.

65. Alcock, "Electronic Voice Phenomena."

66. Quoted in Turner, "Haunted."

67. Guiley, *Encyclopedia of Ghosts and Spirits*, p. 353.

68. Troy Taylor, "Orbs Debunked!" Ghost Research Information and Articles, 2008. www.prairieghosts.com.

69. Quoted in Chris Laursen, "Bachelor's Grove Seeks Single White Apparition," Sue Darroch and Matthew Didier's Paranormal Blog, March 3, 2007. http://seminars.torontoghosts.org.

For Further Research

Books

Jeff Belanger, *The World's Most Haunted Places.* Franklin Lakes, NJ: Career, 2004.

Mary Ellen Guiley, *Encyclopedia of Ghosts and Spirits.* New York: Facts On File, 2009.

Jason Hawes and Grant Wilson, *Ghost Hunting.* New York: Pocket, 2007.

James Van Praagh, *Ghosts Among Us.* New York: HarperCollins, 2008.

Melvyn Willin, *Ghosts Caught on Film.* Newton Abbott, UK: David & Charles, 2007.

Mary Ann Winkowski, *When Ghosts Speak.* New York: Grand Central, 2007.

Internet Sources

John Blake, "When Ghosts Attack," CNN, October 31, 2008. www.cnn.com/2008/LIVING/10/31/boo/index.html.

Ed Grabianowski, "How Ghost Busters Work," How Stuff Works, 2005. http://science.howstuffworks.com/ghost-buster.htm.

Kimberly Turner, "Haunted," *Atlanta Magazine*, October 2008. www.atlantamagazine.com/article.aspx?id=25268.

Tracy V. Wilson, "How Ghosts Work," How Stuff Works, 2007. http://science.howstuffworks.com/ghost.htm.

Web Sites

Discovery Channel Psychic and Paranormal (www.discoverychannel.co.uk/paranormal/index.shtml). Sections of this intriguing site include "The Spirit World," "Most Haunted," "Guide to Ghost Hunting," "Ways to Contact the Dead," and "Paranormal Places," among others.

From the Shadows (http://from-the-shadows.blogspot.com). This blog belongs to Jason Offutt,

74

who is a syndicated columnist, author, college journalism instructor, and "fan of all things strange." It features numerous stories of people's fascinating, and unexplained, experiences with ghostly phenomena.

Ghost Village (www.ghostvillage.com). Dedicated to providing ghost research, evidence, and discussion from around the world, this site features articles about ghostly encounters from 1999 to 2009, ghost chronicles, a news archive, and discussion forums.

Paranormal Phenomena (http://paranormal.about.com/b). Written by Stephen Wagner, a paranormal investigator and author, this blog features a vast collection of stories about ghost sightings, haunted places, and ghost hunting as well as photographs and video and audio clips.

The Atlantic Paranormal Society (TAPS) (www.the-atlantic-paranormal-society.com). This site features an extensive collection of articles as well as a glossary, message boards, videos of the *Ghost Hunters* television show, and a link to "Beyond Reality Radio" that features Jason Hawes and Grant Wilson, TAPS founders and stars on *Ghost Hunters*.

Index

About the Author

Peggy J. Parks holds a bachelor of science degree from Aquinas College in Grand Rapids, Michigan, where she graduated magna cum laude. She has written more than 80 nonfiction books for children and young adults. Parks lives in Muskegon, Michigan, a town that she says inspires her writing because of its location on the shores of Lake Michigan.